BEEF
RECIPES

*Illustrated with
pastoral cattle scenes*

SALMON

Index

Cover pictures *front:* "Driving on to pastures new"
back: "Off to summer pastures"
Title page: "Blossom time"

Printed and Published by J. Salmon Ltd., Sevenoaks, England © Copyright

Steak in Mustard and Cream Sauce

*Ideal for a quick and tasty meal, this recipe needs little preparation
and can be cooked in just a few minutes.*

1 lb. lean rump steak	1 teaspoon Dijon mustard
2 oz. butter	½ pint double cream
2 medium onions, finely chopped	Salt and pepper

Cut the steak into thin strips about 2 inches long. Melt half the butter in a heavy bottomed frying pan, add half the meat and seal on all sides. Remove the meat from the pan, seal the remaining meat and keep all the meat and pan juices aside. (*NB.* the butter and frying pan must be sufficiently hot so that the meat seals quickly. The strips must remain rare inside.) Melt the remaining butter in the pan and gently fry the onions until softened. Stir in half the cream and mix round, incorporating all the juices until the cream begins to thicken. Add the remaining cream, reduce the heat and gradually stir in the mustard, then the meat and all the juices. Thoroughly mix the meat and sauce, season to taste and then serve immediately with rice. Serves 4.

Steak and Kidney Pudding

One of England's best known national dishes.

1 teacup shredded suet	**1½ lb. bladebone steak**
2 teacups self-raising flour	**¼ lb. ox kidney**
Salt and black pepper	**¼ lb. mushrooms**
¼ pint cold water	**1 dozen oysters (optional)**

Mix the flour and suet with seasoning together in a bowl. Add water and mix together to form a soft dough. Cut the meat into small pieces, discarding any gristle or fat. Cut up the kidney after taking out the white core. Cut up the mushrooms. Toss all in seasoned flour. Grease a 1½-2 pint pudding basin. Roll out the suet pastry on a floured surface. Line the basin with two thirds of the paste, reserving one third for the lid. Put the meat, kidney, mushrooms and oysters, if desired, in layers in the basin, sprinkling a little flour with each layer. When the basin is full, add cold water nearly to the brim. Put on a pastry lid, moistening round the edge and pressing down well to make a good seal. Cover the top with greased greaseproof paper, and tie a cloth over it. Put the pudding in a saucepan of boiling water, not more than halfway up the basin. Simmer for three hours. Brown ale can be substituted for water in the pudding; it improves the taste of the gravy! Serves 4-6.

Oxtail Soup

The very long simmering gives this rich brown broth its delicious flavour.

1 lb. oxtail	2 pints beef stock
2 onions	8 peppercorns
2 strips of celery	2 cloves
2 oz. butter	1 medium carrot, grated
2 oz. lean ham or bacon, cut into cubes	1 tablespoon rice
	2 tablespoons barley
1 bay leaf	A small glass of sherry
1 bouquet garni	1 tablespoon cornflour

Roll the oxtail pieces in seasoned flour and fry in a pan, with the butter. Cut the onions and celery into small pieces and add to the pan with the ham or bacon, and fry all together until nicely browned. Add the stock and herbs, peppercorns and cloves; bring to the boil and simmer very gently for 4 hours. Strain and leave to get quite cold, preferably overnight. When cold, take off the fat. Cut up the lean meat of the oxtail into very small pieces and reserve. Put the strained soup into a saucepan and add one medium carrot, grated, the rice and the barley and simmer for 1 hour until the barley is well cooked. Mix the cornflour with the sherry, add to the soup and bring to the boil. Add the oxtail meat last of all, season to taste and continue to cook, to re-heat the oxtail. Serve hot.

Six

Chilli Beef

The amount of chilli powder in this dish can be varied to taste.

2 medium onions, finely chopped	**½ pint beef stock**
1 red pepper, cored and chopped	**1 tin chopped tomatoes**
1 lb. beef mince (best quality)	**½ tablespoon chilli powder**
2 tablespoons oil	**Salt and pepper**

In a heavy based casserole fry the chopped onions and pepper gently in the oil until softened. Add the mince and fry until lightly browned. Add the chilli powder and stir in thoroughly. Cook for about a minute and then add the beef stock and chopped tomatoes. Season to taste, cover and simmer for about 1 hour either on the hotplate or in a pre-heated oven at 350°F or Mark 4 . Check the seasoning and serve with rice or pasta and a green salad. Serves 4.

Beef Olives

Originally known as 'Beef aloes', this is a very old dish
which became particularly popular in the 17th century.

1 to 1½ lb. steak, cut into thin slices	1 bayleaf
4 oz. forcemeat stuffing of your choice	Salt and black pepper
1 oz. lard or 1½ tablespoons oil	1 tablespoon red wine, optional
2 onions, peeled and sliced	Cornflour
1 pint beef stock	1 or 2 bayleaves for garnish

Stretch the steak slices gently, then divide the forcemeat between them. Roll up and secure with fine kitchen string. Heat the fat or oil in a skillet and fry the onion until golden, then add the 'olives' and brown lightly. Add the stock, bayleaf and seasoning, bring to the boil, cover and simmer gently for ¾ to 1 hour or until the meat is tender. Lift out the 'olives' with a draining spoon, remove the string, place on a heated serving dish and keep warm. Add the red wine, if desired, to the liquid in the pan and heat through. Remove the bayleaf, thicken if necessary with a little cornflour and pour over the olives. Serve, garnished with bayleaves and accompanied by creamed potatoes, carrots and a green vegetable. Serves 4-6.

"Cattle at pasture"

West Country Stew

*Doughboy is the Devon name for dumpling. This tasty stew provides
a substantial meal for a winter's day.*

STEW

2 lb. stewing beef   2 medium onions, peeled and diced
2 medium carrots, peeled and sliced   1 small turnip, peeled and diced
½ swede, peeled and diced   2 pints beef stock   2 oz. flour
2 oz. lard or oil/butter mix for frying

DOUGHBOYS

6 oz. flour   4 oz. suet   ½ teaspoon baking powder
Freshly chopped herbs (thyme and parsley)
Salt and pepper   Cold water to mix

Prepare the meat by removing any fat and cutting into cubes. Melt the fat and fry the meat until brown. Add the vegetables and fry for a further few minutes. Stir in the flour and then add the stock, season and simmer in a covered pan for 1-1½ hours. Meanwhile prepare the doughboys by mixing together the flour, suet, baking powder and seasoning. Stir in the herbs and add sufficient water to make a soft dough. Shape into 8-10 small balls and add to the stew; they will swell whilst cooking. Continue cooking for a further 25 minutes or until the meat is tender. Serves 4-6.

Beef Curry

An easy to prepare traditional meat curry.

1 lb. lean beefsteak cut into small cubes or thin strips
1 large onion, finely chopped   2 tablespoons oil
5 fl. oz. plain yoghurt   3 garlic cloves, peeled and crushed
1 teaspoon ground coriander   1 teaspoon ground ginger
1 teaspoon ground cumin   1 teaspoon garam masala powder
1 teaspoon chilli powder   1 tablespoon ground almonds   Salt

Place the meat, yoghurt, garlic, cumin, coriander, garam masala, almonds and ginger in a large bowl. Add a pinch of salt and stir well to mix all the ingredients. Allow to marinate for 1 hour. Heat the oil in a heavy bottomed frying pan or casserole and fry the onion until softened. Add the marinated meat mixture and fry until browned on all sides. Cover and simmer for about 45 minutes (if the mixture becomes too dry a small amount of water can be added). Add the chilli powder and continue to simmer for about 10-15 minutes. Garnish with fresh coriander leaves and serve with rice and nan bread. Serves 4-6.

Steak and Oyster Pie

The flavour of this pie will be improved if the meat filling is cooked the day before.

1 tablespoon cooking oil   1 oz. butter
1½ lb. braising steak, cut into 1 inch cubes
1 medium onion, peeled and diced
2 tablespoons plain flour   ½ pint beef stock   ¼ pint red wine
1 tablespoon tomato purée   ½ teaspoon dried mixed herbs
1 small tin smoked oysters (drained)   8 oz. puff pastry

Set oven to 325°F or Mark 3. Heat the oil in a large frying pan, add the butter and fry the beef in small batches until browned, and transfer to a casserole dish. Fry the onion gently until soft and lightly browned. Stir in the flour and cook for 2 to 3 minutes. Remove from the heat and add the stock, wine, tomato purée and herbs. Return to the heat and, stirring, bring to the boil. Pour over the meat, cover and cook in the oven for 1½ hours. Stir in the oysters and cook for a further 30 minutes. Next, transfer the meat to a 3 pint pie dish and insert a pie funnel in the centre. Roll out the pastry on a lightly floured surface and use to cover the pie dish. Trim and decorate. Increase oven to 425°F or Mark 7. When hot, cook the pie for 25 minutes then reduce oven to 350°F or Mark 4 and cook for a further 15 minutes. Serves 4 to 6.

Pot Roast of Beef

Pot roasting dates back to earliest times. Topside and silverside are ideal for slow cooking in this way as they only have a little fat.

2 lb. joint of beef topside or silverside
2 large onions quartered   6 oz. carrots sliced
1 small swede roughly diced   2 oz. butter   ½ pt. beef stock
¼ pt. red wine   1 clove of garlic crushed   ½ teaspoon dried thyme
Salt and pepper

Melt the butter in a large heavy bottomed casserole and brown the beef joint well on sides. Put to one side and fry the carrots, onions and swede until lightly browned. Place the beef joint on top of the vegetables. Sprinkle the crushed garlic and thyme over the beef, season well and add the stock and wine. Cover the casserole with a lid and work in a pre-heated oven at 350°F or Gas Mark 4 for 1½-2 hours until tender. Remove the lid for the last 30 minutes of cooking to brown the meat. For extra flavour some sliced mushrooms can be added at this stage. Once cooked transfer the joint to a dish for serving and arrange the vegetables round it. The gravy should be served separately. Serve with mashed potatoes and green vegetables. Serves 4-6.

Moussaka

Paprika adds a touch of spiceness to this family favourite.

2 tablespoons olive oil	1 clove of garlic, peeled and crushed
1 lb. best beef mince	2 tablespoons tomato purée
1 medium onion, finely chopped	1 tablespoon paprika
1 large aubergine, sliced thinly	½ pint beef stock
6 oz. mushrooms, chopped	Salt and pepper

TOPPING

1 egg   3 oz. Cheddar cheese grated   5 fl. oz. plain yoghurt

Heat a little of the oil in a large frying pan and fry the aubergine slices in batches on both sides until lightly browned. The slices will tend to absorb the oil, so add a little extra as necessary. Set aside the slices. In the remaining oil fry the onions until softened. Add the mince and stir until thoroughly browned on all sides. Stir in the paprika and mix in well, then add the mushrooms, tomato purée, garlic and stock. Season lightly, cover the pan and simmer for about 15-20 minutes. In a greased ovenproof dish place the aubergine slices and meat sauce in alternate layers starting with the sauce and finishing with aubergine. To make the topping, lightly beat the yoghurt with the egg and incorporate the grated cheese. Spread the topping over the moussaka and bake in a pre-heated oven at 375°F or Mark 5 for about 30-45 minutes. The sauce should be piping hot and the topping nicely browned.

Fifteen

Scouse

Based on the 'soup-stew' concocted by sailors whilst at sea, some versions of Scouse contain pork or mutton as well as beef. It is traditionally eaten with a spoon and fork.

**1 to 2 tablespoons cooking oil or dripping   1½ lb. stewing beef, cubed
Salt and black pepper   1 teaspoon chopped fresh thyme
½ to 1 pint beef stock   3 onions, peeled and chopped
4 carrots, peeled and chopped   1 turnip or swede, peeled and chopped
4 medium potatoes, peeled and quartered**

Heat the oil or dripping in a large saucepan, add the meat and brown quickly. Add the seasoning, thyme and sufficient stock to cover completely. Bring to the boil, then cover and simmer gently for 1 to 1½ hours. Add the vegetables and continue to simmer for another hour. Serve with pickled red cabbage. Serves 4 to 6.

"Beside the pond"

Beef in Stout

A stew that dates from the 19th century, when it was often made with porter, a dark brown ale which, like stout, produced a fine, dark gravy.

1 tablespoon oil	2 tablespoons flour
A walnut of butter	Salt and black pepper
2 lb. stewing steak, wiped and cubed	2 carrots, peeled and sliced
	½ pint stout
2 onions, peeled and sliced	1 teaspoon soft brown sugar

Fresh chopped parsley for garnish

Heat the oil and butter in a large saucepan and cook the meat until lightly browned. Remove with a slotted spoon. Add the onions and fry until softened. Stir in the flour and seasoning, then return the meat to the saucepan with the carrots, stout and sugar. Stir well and bring to the boil, then cover and simmer gently for 2 to 2½ hours or until the meat is tender. Serve garnished with chopped parsley and accompanied by mashed potatoes and a green vegetable. Serves 4 to 6.

If desired, a half-and-half mix of Guinness and water can be used for the gravy and a few sliced mushrooms added to the stew. Alternatively, this dish can be cooked in the oven at 350°F or Mark 4 for the same length of time.

Meat and Potato Pie

*In this steak and kidney pie, a layer of potatoes covers the meat
before finishing with the pastry crust.*

8 oz. shortcrust pastry

FILLING
1 lb. stewing steak and kidney   1 large onion, chopped
1 bayleaf   Salt and pepper   2-3 lb. potatoes
1 tablespoon cornflour

Put the cubed meat, the chopped onion, the bayleaf and seasoning into a saucepan, cover with water and cook, covered, for 2 to 2½ hours until the meat is tender. Peel the potatoes and cut into 1 inch cubes. Put the cubes into a saucepan, add some of the stock from the meat with water to cover and bring to the boil. Cook for 5 minutes. Drain the potatoes and reserve the stock. Set oven to 375°F or Mark 5. Put the meat into a deep pie-dish, cover with the potatoes and moisten with stock. Roll out the pastry larger than the pie-dish and cut a 1 inch strip from around the edge. Place the pastry strip around the edge of the dish and then cover the pie, pressing the edges firmly together and trim. Make a steam hole in the centre. Bake for 30 to 35 minutes. Thicken the unused stock with cornflour to make a gravy, to be served separately. Serves 4-6.

Mince and Tatties

This variation on the plain mince and tatties recipe is full of extra vegetables;
children will never notice!

1 medium onion	2 teaspoons Bovril
1 medium carrot	1 teaspoon redcurrant jelly
2 oz. swede	1 teaspoon tomato purée
1 oz. vegetable oil	1 tablespoon mushroom ketchup
1 lb. best minced beef	1 stick of celery, left whole
Salt and pepper	

Cut the onion, carrot and swede into chunks and put through a food processor until finely chopped. Alternatively they can be well grated by hand. Heat the oil in a saucepan, add the mince and cook for 3 to 4 minutes. Add the finely chopped vegetables and cook for a further 2 to 3 minutes. Add all the other ingredients, including the stick of celery. Cover with water and bring to boiling point. Cover with a lid and simmer for 40 to 45 minutes. When cooked, remove the celery stick. Serve with buttery mashed potato. Serves 4.

Rich Beef Stew

A traditional rich Scottish stew.

1 lb. stewing steak, cubed
A little oil for browning meat
1 large onion, chopped roughly
4 oz. smoked bacon rashers, diced
2 tablespoons oatmeal

¼ small turnip (swede), diced
¼ lb. mushrooms, sliced
2 tablespoons tomato purée
1 teaspoon redcurrant jelly
1 pt. beef stock

5 fl. oz. red wine

First brown the steak on all sides in a little oil in a flameproof casserole, then add the onions and cook for 2 minutes. Add the bacon and cook for a further 2 minutes. Remove from the heat, stir in the oatmeal and then add the diced turnip (swede) and the mushrooms. Add the tomato purée and redcurrant jelly, pour in the stock and wine and stir well. Return to the heat, bring slowly to simmering point, cover and cook slowly for about 1½ to 2 hours until the meat is tender. Check seasoning before serving. Serves 4-6.

Farmhouse Broth

An economical soup given extra flavour by the addition of beef.

6 oz. lean beef, chopped roughly	1 oz. long grain rice
½ oz. butter	½ tablespoon parsley, chopped
4 oz. cooked peas	1 bayleaf
4 oz. potatoes, sliced	1 teaspoon fresh thyme
2 oz. celery, chopped	2 pints water
2 oz. onions, chopped	Salt and pepper

Fry the beef in the butter until browned. Transfer to a large saucepan with the water, bring to the boil and simmer for about 20-30 minutes, skimming regularly. Add all the vegetables, herbs and rice, season with salt and pepper and simmer for about 1½ hours. Remove the bayleaf, liquidise the mixture and serve with crusty farmhouse bread. Serves 4-6.

Beery Beef with Crusty Topping

A delicious, rich stew with a tasty bread topping.

1½ lbs. lean braising beef   2 slices back bacon, chopped   2 tablespoons oil
1 oz. butter   2 tablespoons flour   ½ pint bitter beer   ½ pint beef stock
1 teaspoon caster sugar   2 cloves garlic, peeled and crushed
2 medium onions, skinned and thinly sliced   2 carrots, peeled and sliced
1 bouquet garni   Salt and freshly ground black pepper

TOPPING
6 thick slices of white bread, buttered and spread with 1-2 tablespoons of grainy mustard
3 oz. Cheddar cheese, grated

Set oven to 325°F or Mark 3. Heat the oil and butter together in a frying pan, cut the meat into 1 inch cubes and fry a little at a time until well browned; place in a large casserole dish. Fry the bacon and transfer to the dish. Add the flour to the fat and cook, stirring until lightly browned. Gradually add the beer and stock and stir until the sauce thickens. Add one teaspoon of sugar. Put the garlic, onions and carrots in the casserole dish with the meat and pour the sauce over. Put in the bouquet garni and season with salt and pepper. Cook for 2½ hours until the meat is tender. The casserole will benefit by being stirred half way through cooking. Remove the bouquet garni and arrange the bread on top of the meat. Sprinkle the cheese over and grill until the cheese bubbles. Serves 4-6.

"In the sunken lane"

Farmhouse Pudding

This layered and steamed meat pudding is also known as Wellingborough Hough and Dough Cake – 'hough' being another name for shin of beef.

1 lb. shin of beef, finely diced	1 dessertspoon chopped fresh parsley
2 medium onions, peeled and chopped	1 oz. flour
1 to 2 tablespoons cooking oil	¾ pint beef stock
or 1 oz dripping	Salt and black pepper
3 medium carrots, peeled and grated	1 lb. prepared suet pastry

Mix the meat and onion together. Heat the oil or dripping in a frying pan and fry the meat mixture until brown, then stir in the carrots, parsley and flour. Gradually add the stock and cook, stirring, until the mixture is thick and boiling. Season. Grease a 2 pint pudding basin. Roll out the pastry on a lightly floured surface and cut a circle that will fit the bottom of the basin. Place a layer of meat mixture over this, then add another circle of pastry, continuing to fill the basin with alternate layers, finishing with a circle of pastry. Cover the pudding with greaseproof paper and kitchen foil and seal. Steam for 1 to 1½ hours, topping up the water when necessary. Serve direct from the basin with boiled potatoes and a green vegetable. Serves 4 to 6.

Double Crust Pie

A double crust pie has a base as well as a covering of pastry.

1 lb. best beef mince	1 oz. flour
1 large onion, sliced	½ teaspoon curry powder
2 oz. mushrooms, sliced	½ pint beef stock
1 egg, beaten	Shortcrust pastry
1 tablespoon oil	Salt and pepper

In a frying pan soften the onions in the oil. Add the beef mince and fry until lightly browned. Add the mushrooms, stir in the curry powder and flour and cook for a further 2-3 minutes. Add the beef stock, season and simmer for about 15-20 minutes until the liquid has reduced somewhat. Line a 1 pint pie dish with pastry and put in the meat mixture. Cover with pastry, seal around the edges and brush the top with beaten egg. Bake in a hot oven at 425°F or Mark 7 for 30 minutes until the pastry is golden, then reduce the temperature to 350°F or Mark 4 and cook for a further 15 minutes. Serves 4.

Beef Stew with Walnuts

A rich stew from Berkshire.

1 lb. stewing steak	2 sprigs thyme and 4 sprigs
1 oz. dripping	parsley, tied together with string
1 onion, peeled and sliced	12 button mushrooms, wiped
2 fl. oz. red wine	2 oz. chopped walnuts
1 pint beef stock	1 stick of celery, trimmed and chopped
Salt and black pepper	½ oz. butter

A little grated orange peel for garnish

Cut the steak into 2 inch cubes, dust with a little seasoned flour and fry in the dripping until lightly browned. Remove with a slotted spoon and fry the onion in the residual dripping until golden. Return the meat to the pan and add the wine, stock, *bouquet garni* and seasoning. Bring to the boil, then cover and simmer for 1½ to 2 hours. Fry the mushrooms, walnuts and celery in the butter and add to the stew after 1 hour of cooking. Remove the herbs and transfer the stew to a heated serving dish. Serve, garnished with grated orange peel and accompanied by creamed potatoes and a green vegetable. Serves 4.

"Returning from the fields"

Steak and Kidney Pie

Rump steak gives this traditional pie its distinctive flavour.

12 oz. shortcrust pastry   2 lb. rump steak, trimmed and cut into 2 inch cubes
1 lb. ox or veal kidney, skinned, cored and cut into thin slices
Seasoned flour for dusting   3 oz. butter   1 large onion, peeled and sliced
½ lb. mushrooms, sliced   2 sprigs thyme and a bayleaf, tied together with string
2 level dessertspoons chopped fresh parsley   Salt and black pepper
Pinch dry mustard powder   1 pint rich brown stock   ½ teaspoon Worcestershire Sauce
1 teaspoon lemon juice   2 tablespoons red wine (optional)

Set oven to 325°F or Mark 3. Dust meat with seasoned flour. Melt butter in a large frying pan and cook onion until soft. Add steak and kidney and brown lightly. Arrange steak and kidney in layers, with onion, in a 3 pint pie dish, placing mushrooms on top. Add thyme and bayleaf. Put all remaining ingredients, including wine (if used), in pan and bring to boil, stirring. Pour into dish. Cover with foil and cook for 1 to 1½ hours or until meat is tender. Allow to cool completely. Set oven to 400°F or Mark 6. Roll out pastry, remove herbs, cover pie, trim pastry; press down well. Decorate, and make small steam hole. Brush with milk or beaten egg. Bake for 15 minutes, reduce oven temperature to 350°F or Mark 4 and bake for further 20 to 30 minutes, or until pastry is golden brown. Serve with potatoes and vegetables. Serves 4 to 8.

Liver and Onion Pie

The combination of liver and onions dates from medieval times.

1½ lb. ox liver
2 lbs. onions sliced into rings
2 oz. butter
½ teaspoon chopped thyme

½ teaspoon chopped rosemary
1 oz. flour (seasoned)
¾ pint beef stock
1 lb. shortcrust pastry

Melt the butter in a large frying pan and cook the onions slowly until soft and golden. Place half the onions in the bottom of a large pie dish. Cut the liver into thin strips about 3 inches long, cutting out any gristle or fat and toss in the seasoned flour. Place a layer of liver over the onions and sprinkle over the herbs. Cover with more onions and then repeat the layers of liver and onions finishing with a layer of onions. Add the stock until it just covers the liver and onions. Roll out the pastry quite thickly and cover the pie dish, sealing the edges carefully. Bake at the top of a pre-heated oven at 400°F or Gas Mark 6 for about 20 minutes, then cover the crust lightly with foil and cook for a further 60 minutes on a lower shelf.

Spiced Beef

Eaten hot or cold, Spiced Beef is traditionally served on Christmas Day or Boxing Day, decorated with holly.

4 lb. rolled salted silverside	**12 cloves**
1 onion, sliced	**2 oz. soft brown sugar**
1 small turnip, sliced	**Juice of 1 lemon**
3 carrots, sliced	**½ teaspoon each ground cinnamon,**
1 bayleaf	**allspice and nutmeg**
Water, stout or brown ale	**1 level teaspoon mustard powder**

Soak the meat in cold water overnight. Next day, rinse well and tie up with kitchen string to form a firm, neat joint. Put the onion, turnip and carrots in a large saucepan, place the meat on top, add the bayleaf then cover with cold water or a mixture of water and stout or brown ale. Bring to the boil, skim, then cover and simmer gently for 3½ to 4 hours. Leave to cool completely in the liquid. Set oven to 350°F or Mark 4. Drain the meat very well, place in a roasting tin and stick with the cloves. Mix together all the remaining ingredients and spread over the meat. Bake for 40 minutes, basting from time to time. Remove the string and serve hot or cold. Serves 4 to 6.

"In the meadow"

Beef Pasties

A conveniently portable meal which can be eaten hot or cold.

1½ lbs. shortcrust pastry

FILLING
1 lb. braising steak, trimmed and coarsely minced or cut into small pieces
8 oz. potatoes, peeled and diced   4 oz. turnip, peeled and finely diced
1 medium onion, peeled and diced
Salt   Freshly ground black pepper

Set oven to 425°F or Mark 7. Mix together the filling ingredients in a bowl and season well. Divide the pastry into 8 pieces and roll out on a lightly floured surface into rounds about 8 inches in diameter (use a saucepan lid as a cutter). Divide the filling equally between the pastry rounds and damp the edges with water. Fold the pastry over and seal well, fluting the edges with the fingers. Place on a lightly floured baking sheet and cook for 20 minutes; reduce oven to 350°F or Mark 4 and cook for a further 45 minutes, covering the pasties with greaseproof paper if they begin to brown too much.

Beef Provençale

A rich beef casserole flavoured with wine, garlic and herbs.

1½ lbs. stewing steak	½ pint red wine
2 medium carrots, chopped	2 tablespoons olive oil
2 medium onions, sliced	½ pint beef stock
2 cloves of garlic, crushed	Bouquet garni
3 oz. button mushrooms	Strip of orange peel
1 tin chopped tomatoes	A dozen black olives (pitted)
2 rashers streaky bacon, chopped	Salt and pepper

1 tablespoon fresh parsley, chopped

Cut the steak into cubes, place in a large bowl and stir in the wine, olive oil, beef stock and orange peel. Marinate for 2-3 hours. In a heavy bottomed casserole fry the bacon in a little oil, then add the carrots, onions, mushrooms, garlic, parsley and tomatoes. Stir well and cook gently for 10 minutes. Season and then add the meat and marinade and the bouquet garni. Bring to the boil, then cover and cook slowly in a pre-heated oven at 300°F or Mark 2 for about 3 hours. About half an hour before the end of the cooking time stir in the olives. Remove the bouquet garni and orange peel and serve. Serves 4-6.

Braised Beef and Mushrooms

Port wine adds richness to this simple casserole dish.

1 lb. chuck steak cut into 2 inch pieces	**2 wineglasses of port wine**
1½ oz. butter	**½ teaspoon mixed herbs**
½ lb. small onions, chopped	**1 bayleaf**
1 tablespoon flour	**Salt and pepper**
½ pint beef stock or water	**½ lb. flat mushrooms**

Set oven to 350°F or Mark 4. In a flameproof casserole dish, melt 1 oz. of the butter and brown the meat on all sides. Remove from the dish and set aside. Melt the remaining butter in the casserole and cook the chopped onions for a few minutes. Stir in the flour, blend in the stock and continue stirring until boiling. Return the steak to the pan and add the port wine, herbs and bayleaf, and season with salt and pepper. Stir until boiling. Put the lid on the casserole and cook in the oven for 1½ hours or until the meat is tender. Slice the mushrooms and add to the casserole; cover again and cook for a further ½ hour. Serves 4.

Beef with Chestnuts

A rich, winter stew from the county of Surrey.

15-20 chestnuts   1 large onion, peeled and sliced   2 lb. stewing steak, cubed
Seasoned flour for dusting   1 oz. butter
½ pint beef stock, or ¼ pint stock and ¼ pint red wine mixed
Salt and black pepper   Pinch of ground nutmeg

Set oven to 325°F or Mark 3. Split the skins of the chestnuts and cook them in hot water for about 5 minutes, then, whilst still warm, remove the outer skins and the inner membranes. Dust the steak with seasoned flour. Melt the butter in a frying pan and fry the onion until soft. Add the steak and brown lightly on all sides. Put the steak and the onions in an ovenproof casserole. Add the stock, or stock and red wine, seasoning and the nutmeg, then stir in the chestnuts. Cover and cook for 1½ hours or until the meat is tender. Serve with braised celery. Serves 4-6.

Spicy Beef with Tomatoes

Beef and tomatoes combine well in this rich curry.

1 lb. braising steak, cut into cubes	1½ teaspoons ground ginger
1 medium onion, finely chopped	1 teaspoon ground coriander
2 tablespoons oil	1½ teaspoons ground cumin
1 can of chopped tomatoes	½ teaspoon ground tumeric
3 garlic cloves, peeled and crushed	1 teaspoon chilli powder

Salt

Heat the oil in a heavy bottomed frying pan or casserole and fry the onion until softened. Add the meat, garlic, tumeric, ginger, cumin and coriander. Coat the meat with all the spices and fry gently until lightly browned (about 10 minutes). Season with a little salt, add the chilli powder and tomatoes, cover and simmer for about 1 hour. Garnish with some segments of fresh tomatoes and serve with rice, nan or poppadoms. Serves 4.

Lasagne

Historically, this sauce requires lengthy cooking, which is why restaurants and rural homes in Italy allow it to simmer on the wood stove for as much as a couple of hours. On a modern cooker, you can happily make do with average cooking of 45 minutes

**1 lb. green lasagne   12 oz. minced beef   A small onion   A stick of celery
1 carrot   A cup of tomato sauce   4 oz. reggio Parmesan
Butter, flour and milk to prepare the white sauce
Salt, pepper and extra virgin olive oil, butter**

Finely chop the vegetables and lightly fry in extra virgin olive oil, together with the minced meat, the tomato sauce, the salt and pepper. Stir frequently. Meanwhile prepare approx ½ pint of white sauce. When the meat sauce is ready, cook the lasagne in plenty of salted, boiling water. Drain off and place the sheets on a linen cloth. Place a layer of the meat sauce, topped by the white creamed sauce, in a buttered oven dish. Cover with a layer of lasagne and so continue until all the ingredients have been used. Cover with white cream sauce and some flakes of butter. Then cook in the oven at medium heat at a temperature of approx. 325°F or Gas Mark 3 for about 20 minutes until the surface is golden. Serve in the oven dish at the table. Serves 4-6.

"A quiet drink"

Boiled Beef

A warming meal made with the famous Maldon Sea Salt.

1 piece of topside or silverside of beef	**Bunch of herbs**
1 carrot	**2 cloves**
1 onion, peeled	**Peppercorns**
1 leek	**Water**

Maldon Crystal Salt

Peel the onion and stud with the cloves. Scrub the carrot, wash the leek and place with the meat and all the other ingredients, except the salt, in a saucepan. Cover with water, bring to the boil and simmer until the meat is cooked and tender. Lift the meat out of the stock on to a serving dish. Serve the meat sliced, with a good grinding of Maldon Crystal Sea Salt over each slice, together with accompanying vegetables. The stock can be used for soup. Serves 4.

Jugged Steak

A simple, but delicious recipe that has its origins in the cauldron cookery of the Middle Ages, when a number of different dishes were boiled together in one large pot.

1½ to 2 lb. rump steak	**Salt and black pepper**
1 onion, peeled and left whole	**1 or 2 teaspoons mushroom ketchup**
10 cloves	**3 sprigs parsley and a small bayleaf,**
2 carrots, peeled and diced	**tied together with string**
2 sticks celery, trimmed and diced	

Cut the steak into small, neat cubes and place in a tall narrow casserole that has been rinsed out in cold water. Stick the onion with the cloves and add to the meat. Rinse the carrots and celery in cold water, drain well and add to the meat. Season, then add the mushroom ketchup and *bouquet garni*. Do not add any fat, stock or water. Cover the casserole with a piece of kitchen foil and place the lid firmly on top. Place in a saucepan of boiling water and stew for 2 hours, topping up the water as necessary. Before serving, discard the herbs and the cloves from the onion and then slice the onion and return it to the casserole. Serve with boiled potatoes and a green vegetable. Serves 4 to 6.

Forfar Bridies

Steak pasties which can be eaten hot or cold.

1 lb. Shortcrust pastry	3 oz. shredded suet
12 oz. best stewing steak	¼ teaspoon mustard powder
1 medium onion, chopped finely	Salt and pepper

Beaten egg to glaze

Set oven to 350°F or Mark 4. Chop the meat into very small pieces or mince coarsley. Place in a bowl with the chopped onion, salt, pepper and mustard. Sprinkle on the suet and mix well. Cut the pastry into 3 pieces and roll out each piece to a round about ¼ inch thick. Spoon the meat on to one half of each round, taking care not to overfill. Dampen the edges of the pastry, fold to make semi-circles and pinch the edges together to resemble small Cornish pasties. Place on a plain baking sheet. Brush with beaten egg and make a hole in each one for the steam to escape. Bake for about 1¼ hours until golden brown; if the pastry browns too quickly, cover with foil. Serve hot with vegetables or cold as a snack.

The rustic bridge"

Welsh Beef Stew

This all-in-one stew would sometimes be used to provide two meals;
meat and vegetables for one and broth for another.

1 oz. butter
1½ lb. stewing steak, cubed
8 oz. streaky bacon rashers,
   de-rinded and cut into four
1 tablespoon flour
1½ to 2 pints water
2 onions, peeled and sliced
2 carrots, peeled and sliced

2 small turnips, peeled and cubed
1 heaped dessertspoon fresh chopped
   herbs (parsley, thyme, sage, etc. mixed)
Salt and white pepper
¼ pint cider
½ lb. potatoes, weighed after peeling
3 leeks, washed and trimmed
Chopped fresh parsley for garnish

Melt the butter in a large saucepan and fry the beef and bacon lightly, then sprinkle over the flour and fry for a further minute. Add the water and bring to the boil, then cover and simmer for 40 minutes. Allow to cool slightly and skim, then add the onions, carrots and turnips, herbs and seasoning and bring to the boil. Add the cider, cover and simmer for 1 hour. Add the potatoes and leeks, cover and simmer for a further 20 to 30 minutes. Serve, sprinkling each portion with a little finely chopped parsley. Serves 4 to 6.

Durham Cutlets

A recipe for using up left-over cooked beef, shaped into cutlets and fried in breadcrumbs.
Traditionally, Durham Cutlets were decorated with paper cutlet frills.

1 lb. cooked beef	**Salt and black pepper**
1 onion, peeled and finely chopped	**1 teaspoon brown sauce**
½ oz. butter	**1 egg, lightly beaten**
3 oz. fresh white breadcrumbs	**Egg and breadcrumbs for coating**
Grated rind of half a lemon	**Oil for frying**
1 dessertspoon chopped fresh parsley	**Macaroni pieces**
Pinch of nutmeg	**Chopped fresh parsley for garnish**

Mince the beef. Fry the onion in the butter until soft, then mix with the beef in a bowl. Stir in the breadcrumbs, lemon rind, parsley, nutmeg, seasoning and brown sauce and combine well. Add sufficient beaten egg to bind, then, on a lightly floured surface, form the mixture into traditional 'cutlet' shapes. Brush with beaten egg and coat with breadcrumbs. Heat the oil and fry the 'cutlets' until golden brown. Drain on kitchen paper and keep warm. Just before serving, insert a piece of macaroni into the end of each cutlet to represent the 'bone' and serve garnished with chopped parsley and accompanied by creamed potatoes and a green vegetable. Serves 4.

METRIC CONVERSIONS

The weights, measures and oven temperatures used in the preceding recipes can be easily converted to their metric equivalents. The conversions listed below are only approximate, having been rounded up or down as may be appropriate.

Weights

Avoirdupois	Metric
1 oz.	just under 30 grams
4 oz. (¼ lb.)	app. 115 grams
8 oz. (½ lb.)	app. 230 grams
1 lb.	454 grams

Liquid Measures

Imperial	Metric
1 tablespoon (liquid only)	20 millilitres
1 fl. oz.	app. 30 millilitres
1 gill (¼ pt.)	app. 145 millilitres
½ pt.	app. 285 millilitres
1 pt.	app. 570 millilitres
1 qt.	app. 1.140 litres

Oven Temperatures

	°Fahrenheit	Gas Mark	°Celsius
Slow	300	2	150
	325	3	170
Moderate	350	4	180
	375	5	190
	400	6	200
Hot	425	7	220
	450	8	230
	475	9	240

Flour as specified in these recipes refers to plain flour unless otherwise described.